MOMMY &
DADDY ARE
GETTING
DIVORCED

HELPING CHILDREN COPE
WITH DIVORCE

Dr. Kristine Turner, Ph.D.

A Books To Believe In Publication
All Rights Reserved
Copyright 2010 by Kristine Turner

Proudly Published in the USA by
Thornton Publishing, Inc
17011 Lincoln Ave. #408
Parker, CO 80134

Phone: (303)-794-8888
Fax: (720)-863-2013

BooksToBelieveIn.com
publisher@bookstobelievein.com

ISBN: 0-9845417-5-6

DivorceAdviceForChildren.com

Cataloguing in Publication Data
is on file with the Library of Congress

Dedication

This book is dedicated to my children.

K.C. Conner, McKinzie, and Kylie,
you make life exciting
and new everyday.

Prologue

I was inspired to write this book years ago when I went through my own divorce. My children were young at the time, and I wanted them to have a book that dealt with the emotional aspects of divorce from a child's perspective. As a clinical psychologist in private practice since 1994, I decided that the best way to share my expertise as well as my experience with divorce was through books and seminars. This children's book gives both adults and children an overview of the normal feelings that accompany divorce and what to do with those powerful emotions.

There is a sadness in the house.

Mommy and Daddy are getting a divorce.

That means that Daddy is going to have a home and Mommy is going to find a separate place to live. You and your brothers and/or sisters, if you have them, are probably going to live at both houses.

You will spend some of your time with Mommy and some of your time with Daddy. You may wonder what it will be like to live in two different places. You may wonder if you will miss your Mommy when you are at Daddy's house. You may wonder if Daddy will miss you when you are at Mommy's house.

It might feel like it is too much to think about, and you may wish that you could just go to bed and forget about it.

You will have days when you want to wake up in the morning and have everything go back to the way it used to be before Daddy and Mommy decided to get divorced.

You may have thought to yourself, "If I wish really hard for this yucky feeling to go away, maybe it will be gone in the morning."

So, you go to sleep, but when you wake up the next morning, although it's a sunny day outside, you don't feel happy.

As a matter of fact, you feel weird inside. You can't believe that your life is going to change so much.

You probably don't like when Mommy and Daddy fight, but you might want Daddy and Mommy to stay together and you might wish that life would feel "normal" again.

You may not like the change that is happening in your family. You may want to pretend that everything will go back to the way it used to be for you and your family.

After a couple of months you might start to feel angry with your parents.

You might be mad at your Mommy for letting Daddy leave, or you might be mad at Daddy for getting a new home.

You might get mad at your friends;

or get mad at your teachers, or even get mad at the dog.

You might feel mad about everything, but mostly you are angry because you can't bring your family back together. Your parents are going to get a divorce no matter how angry you get.

It may seem like you will never be happy again, and that you have no control over your life.

You may try being really bad to get the attention off of the divorce and onto yourself.

You may be tempted to quit doing your homework, or start playing with the mean kids on the play ground.

You may even get into a fight with your best friend, but no matter how many times your parents have to come talk to the teacher at school, they will still move forward with their divorce.

Sometimes kids try being really good.

You might try helping cook dinner, or taking out the trash, you might even volunteer to play with your younger sister, or brother, but no matter how good or how bad you are, nothing is going to put Mommy and Daddy back together again.

Your Mommy or Daddy might tell you that no matter how good or how bad you act, that Mommy and Daddy will always love you, but that they don't love each other anymore and that they have made an adult decision to get a divorce.

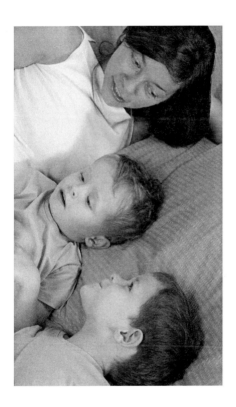

There is nothing you can do to change their minds. The divorce wasn't your fault, it was the adult's decision. You can't do anything to change the situation. Although you might feel disappointed, you will also realize that you have to get used to your parent's divorce.

At this point, you might start to feel really sad.

You might feel like you want to cry all the time. You will need someone to talk to about all the yucky emotions you are having inside.

Sometimes schools have teachers and counsellors that can help you feel better.

These people will explain that many kids have families who are going through divorce. The counselor might meet with you every week for a little while to talk about what it feels like to have your mommy and daddy go through a divorce.

A counsellor or teacher may also say that it will help make you feel better if you talk about the sadness and the anger that you are feeling inside.

You might find that your grandmother, grandfather, or another family relative or coach may have more time to talk than your parents.

You might decide to talk to one of them about what has happened at school that day, or about how you feel about the divorce.

You might find that grandma is a good listener, and that she can talk about the yucky family stuff that is going on right now. As luck would have it, most grandmas and grandpas are good at listening, and they may tell you that you can talk to them any time you need to talk.

It will take time for things to feel better inside.

But as time goes by, you will start to feel normal again.

You will notice that your grades might get better in school again, you might start wanting to play with your friends again, you will start feeling happy again. You will also notice that your parents aren't fighting so much any more, and that the family seems to be getting used to living in two separate homes.

It won't be such a big deal if your parents run into each other at the store; and the little things won't seem to bug them so much anymore. Mommy will be happier in her new life, and Daddy will be happier in his life.

Slowly but surely, things will return to "normal" again. You will start to feel normal too.

Eventually, you will feel comfortable with the families' new situation.

Although it will have been a rough year or two, you will have learned that you have a strong family that can survive tough times.

You will also learn that it is important to talk about your feelings with other people when you are hurting inside. You will learn that many children go through divorce, and that there are a lot of adults who will help when times are rough.

Most of all, you will learn that if you work hard to get through something challenging you can succeed, and you can feel hopeful and happy again.

The Five Stages of Grief

The five stages of grief usually take a year or more to successfully traverse. Parents will lead their children through these emotional stages, children will not be ahead of their parents emotionally. Parents can be in different stages of grief from one another, and they will be ahead of their children in moving through the emotional processes of divorce. Give yourself and your family time to accept this change in their lives.

Parents must reach acceptance
for kids to reach acceptance.

DENIAL is the initial period of not accepting the reality of the divorce or loss. It is a natural defense that allows one enough time to accept what is happening. You may feel numb or in shock. You may say for instance, "This can't be happening to me or my family." Children may find themselves saying, "My mom's not gone, she's on a business trip."

ANGER is an intense feeling of rage, envy or resentment, and may be targeted at innocent bystanders, (i.e., your children). Often you feel angry about being let down and you may act out feelings in a variety of inappropriate ways. Finding an acceptable way to express your anger is an integral part of the healing process. Remember, anger is normal in divorce situations.

BARGAINING is a period of wanting to fix things that are beyond your control. It's rethinking your decision to divorce. You might say something like, "If only I had done such and such..." Often we feel guilt for what has happened and may blame ourselves. Children may think the divorce is their fault and may act really good or really bad in order to take the attention off of the divorce and place it onto themselves assuming that then you will get back together.

DEPRESSION occurs when the reality of the loss sets in. At this stage you may feel despair. You may question your ability to deal with your sadness and may turn to unhealthy coping devices to ease your pain. Overeating, sleep disorders, excessive alcohol consumption, and drugs are all manifestations of a depressed state. During this stage, you need nurturing and support and need healthy ways to live with your sadness and to overcome any unrealistic guilt you may feel.

ACCEPTANCE is the final stage of grief. It is a time when change is no longer a threat. Depending upon the circumstances, you might be more optimistic about the future, or more accepting of your present circumstances.

Key Points To Remember

A. It is not uncommon for parents to be in separate stages.

B. Children always follow their parents through these stages; therefore, children cannot get to acceptance unless one of their parents does.

C. Going through these stages is a necessary process towards healing that may or may not go in this exact order.

Useful Tips for Helping Your Children More Effectively Deal With Divorce

1. Listen to your children. Spend time sitting quietly with your children, allowing them to talk about their day and their feelings. Make eye contact with them.

2. Reassure your children that you will be available to them.

3. Show your children, through your actions, that you are trustworthy.

4. Reassure your children that they will continue to have a relationship with both parents.

5.   Continue to set limits and discipline your children, as structure is helpful to them.

6.   Encourage children to express their feelings, (including sadness, loss, hurt, anger, guilt, helplessness, or fear) even if what they say is hard to hear.

7.   Encourage children to express their opinions.

8.   Demonstrate your love on a daily basis.

9.   Explain changes in concrete terms. Show them where each parent will live, reassure them that there will be enough food, and

money. Don't bother them with the details, refrain from sharing concerns about finances or residences with them.

10. Try to use a business-like communication model with the other parent in order to discuss the needs of your children.

11. Develop a workable parenting plan.

12. Help children adapt to both of their homes, e.g. toothbrush, clothes, toys, books, at both homes.

13. Keep both parents involved.

14. Keep children out of the middle.

Tips For Children Coping With Divorce

1.   Understand that it is not your fault. Your parent's arguments and divorce are not your fault and are not under your control.

2.   You don't need to solve your parents problems. Parents shouldn't ask you to take sides, relay messages or keep secrets. If they do, tell them that you would prefer to stay out of the situation.

3.   Leave the room when your parents argue.

4.   Understand that going through a divorce is hard on everyone. Many families have parents who divorce, and the confusing, sad, or scary feelings you may be experiencing are normal and will eventually go away.

5.   Try to express your feelings. Talk to someone you can trust.

6.   Ask your parents for the things you may need, such as time together; to be kept out of the middle of the divorce; to be trusted if you don't want to talk at the moment; to be allowed to love the other parent; to be allowed to express all kinds of feelings, even if it may hurt your parents.

7.   Remember, every person gets angry at times, and you are not terrible for having angry thoughts and feelings even toward your parents.

8.   Having angry "thoughts" toward someone will not cause that person harm.

9.   Remember, the best thing you can do for yourself is act your age. Don't go back to being a baby, and don't try to be too grown-up.

10. If your parents try to win you over to their side of the story; tell them you want to be free to love both of your parents.

11. Don't take sides against one of your parents. It will make it much harder to develop a bond with the parent you alienated.

12. Keep in mind that although your parents are no longer husband and wife, they will always be your mom and dad.

Recommended Reading

Mom's House Dad's House   Issolina Ricci

This book provides parents and children with an overview of what life looks like in two separate households. It includes suggestions for parenting plans, and coparenting arrangements broken down by age group and developmental stage.

ISBN: 0743277120

Parents Are Forever   Shirley Thomas

This book is helpful to parents who are newly separated, and gives a broad overview of what to expect in the divorce process for families.   ISBN: 0964637839

Rebuilding, When Your Relationship Ends   Bruce Fisher

Readers will gain insight into rebuilding yourself emotional as you travel through the divorce process. The typical stages of grief are highlighted and coping mechanisms as well as particle techniques for regaining control of your life after divorce are ISBN: 1886230692

Dinosaur's Divorce   Marc Brown & Laurene Krasny Brown

One of the first books ever written for children going through divorce, this remains a classic for younger children whose parents are going through divorce.   ISBN: 0316109967

Let's Talk About Divorce   Fred Rogers

Written by Mr. Rogers, himself, this book on divorce uses photographs to depict the typical feelings and questions your child might have as the family goes through the divorce process.   ISBN: 0698116704

My Family's Changing   Pat Thomas
This is a practical guide for younger children about what to expect when your parents decide to divorce. Questions are inserted throughout the book to help children express their feelings.   ISBN: 0764109952

It's Not Your Fault Koko Bear   Vicki Lansky
This book follows the story of Koko Bear through the emotional stages of divorce.   ISBN: 0916773477

The Boys and Girls book about Divorce (teens)
Richard Gardner, M.D.
This guide is written for older children (tweens and teens). It discusses the emotions around divorce ad what to do with them. It provides productive coping mechanisms for older children and teens to use when they are angry or sad. This book helps to answer   ISBN: 0553276190

Good Karma Divorce   Michele Lowrance
The Good Karma Divorce helps readers understand how to "Avoid Litigation, Turn Negative Emotions into Positive Actions, and Get On with the Rest of Your Life   ISBN: 0061840696

Divorce is Not the End of the World   Zoe and Evan Stern
Many kids are experiencing divorce and Zoe and Evan have ritten this firsthand guide to help other kids deal with: their feelings of guilt, madness, sadness, and fear; adjusting to different rules at different houses; birthdays and other holidays as wells stepparents and blended families.   ISBN: 1883672449

About
Kristine Turner, Ph.D.

Dr. Turner has worked with divorcing parents for more than 15 years and has, as a mother, personally experienced divorce as well - which inspired her to write this book to the parents of divorce, to read to the children of divorce.

One of the original founders of New Beginnings, Dr. Turner has acted as the director of the New Beginnings Parenting After Divorce programs since 1995.

Over the years, Dr. Turner has worked with thousands of parents and families going through divorce.

Dr. Kristine Turner is a clinical psychologist, licensed in the state of Colorado. She received her doctorate from the Pacific Graduate School of Psychology, an APA accredited school, in 1994.

THE GUIDE TO A SMART DIVORCE
EXPERTS' ADVICE FOR SURVIVING DIVORCE

KRISTINE TURNER, PH.D.
JAN PARSONS, SENIOR MORTGAGE BANKER
KIM LANGELAAR, CDFA™
DAVID W. HECKENBACH, ESQ.
KURT GROESSER, BROKER ASSOCIATE, MBA

Been There, Done That - authors who specialize in the field of divorce and have experienced it themselves tell you the best ways to handle the difficult situations you're facing.

www.DivorceAdvice360.com

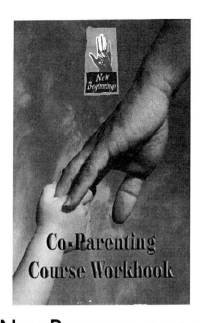

NEW BEGINNINGS FOR DIVORCING PARENTS

CO-PARENTING DIVORCE WORKBOOK

DR. KRISTINE TURNER, PH.D

A divorce co-parenting workbook to help you understand the inner workings of how a child interprets divorce and what is normal and what is not normal and how to handle both situations.

Statistics, tips, suggestions and genuine help to get you through this trying time in your life, so that when it is over, you will be able to heal quickly and with as much grace as possible.

ISBN: 0-9845417-3-X

ORDER FORM
Mommy and Daddy Are Getting Divorced

$12.97 + 2.50 (S&H)

online at:
http://DivorceAdviceForChildren.com

by phone:
have your credit card handy and call:
(303) 794-8888

by fax:
(303) 814-3180

by mail:
send check payable to:
New Beginnings
558 Castle Pines Pkwy
Unit B4 PMB 364
Castle Rock, CO 80108

ISBN: 0-9845417-5-6

Name: _____

Address _____

_____

Phone: _____

E-mail: _____

Credit Card #: _____

Card Type: _____   Expiration Date: ___ / ___

Security Code: _____